The American Poetry Series

Volume 1—*Radiation,* Sandra McPherson
Volume 2—*Boxcars,* David Young

Radiation

Sandra McPherson

The Ecco Press New York

First published in 1973 by The Ecco Press
1 West 30 Street, New York, N.Y. 10001
Published simultaneously in Canada by
The Macmillan Company of Canada Limited
Distributed by The Viking Press, Inc.
SBN 912-94604-0
Library of Congress catalog card number: 73-81356
Printed in U.S.A.

The italicized line in Section V of "Water Poems" is a line of Trumbull Stickney's. Reprinted with the permission of Farrar, Straus & Giroux, Inc., from *The Poems of Trumbull Stickney*, edited and with an introduction by Amberys R. Whittle. © 1966, 1969, 1972 by Amberys R. Whittle. The italicized material in "Collapsars" is slightly modified from its source in *Natural History* magazine.

Grateful acknowledgment is made to the following magazines, in which some of the poems in this book were first published. *Field:* "Three from the Market," "Selective Letter," "Collapsars." *Harper's Magazine:* "Cinderella." *The Iowa Review:* "Homage to John Clare," "Letter with a Black Border," "A Feast for Rats: Old Japanese Print." *Malahat Review:* "Butchery." *The Nation:* "Peddler," "Coin." *New American Review:* "Three Hard Sonnets." *The New Republic:* "Peter Rabbit," "Wanting a Mummy," "Sonnet for Joe." *Poetry:* "Holding Pattern," "Some Meanings of Silence," "The War Surplus Store," "Siberia," "Eschatology," "Seaweeds," "Some Engravings of Pierre Joseph Redouté." *Poetry Northwest:* "A Pumpkin at New Year's." *Shenandoah:* "Raffaele Minichiello."

This book would not have been possible without the encouragement of the Ingram Merrill Foundation.

Also by Sandra McPherson
Elegies for the Hot Season

For my father and mother

Contents

Holding Pattern *1*
Some Meanings of Silence *4*
The War Surplus Store *6*
Three Hard Sonnets *8*
Homage to John Clare *11*
Three from the Market *14*
A Pumpkin at New Year's *18*
Selective Letter *20*
Letter with a Black Border *22*
Raffaele Minichiello *24*
Marlow and Nancy *26*
Butchery *27*
Peter Rabbit *30*
Cinderella *32*
Sisters *34*
Peddler *36*
Coin *38*
Siberia *40*
Eschatology *45*
Poem for Ishi, the Last Wild Indian *46*
Water Poems *48*
Seaweeds *52*
Some Engravings of Pierre Joseph Redouté *53*

Ballad of Sonnets 56
Wanting a Mummy 58
Collapsars 60
A Feast for Rats: Old Japanese Print 66
Sonnet for Joe 67

RADIATION

The color of a thing is that one which, out of all the colors, it repels and cannot assimilate. High heaven refuses blue, returning azure to the retina. All summer long the leaves hold in the red. Charcoal gobbles all.

To our senses things offer only their rejections. We know them by their refuse. Perfume is what the flowers throw away.

Perhaps we only know other people by what they eliminate, by what their substance will not accept. If you are good, it is because you retain your evil. If you blaze, hurling off sparkles and lightnings, your sorrow, gloom, and stupidity keep house within you. They are more you, more yours, than your brilliance. Your genius is everything you are not. Your best deeds are those most foreign to you.

—Paul Valéry

Holding Pattern

For Sister Madeline DeFrees and Sister Michele Birch

Poetry is a way of counting,
                    sisters,
                                it is acquisitive.
I try to find something to hold on to,
                        laid up in heaven.
Held down,
            ill at ease,
                        but blameless,
                                    I meet no one in the air,
In terrible anticipation to walk
                        with you,
                                    paper-soled
Women,
            into the brick learning places
                        and open-windowed rooms.
So it is eternal—
                this aught
                            that we believe to be a high
Degree of order
                with the controlled
                            suspense of the sun.

As I circle you

   you hold your crosses

      sacred, those four

Straight routes

   that draw off pain

      and that lightning

Body they ground.

    I began with a line

      hardly a pardonable

Sin in my book.

   How much should you see

      of yourself,

       or say?

Sometimes I want to be told

    what is great.

      "We have developed

A slight technical difficulty

    and may not be able to land

Without a mechanic."

    We are in the habit of writing,

      and any

Power
      we may derive from each other's company
                        will circle quietly
Over the page,
         complicated as what we don't see
                    but the pilot knows.
In whatever space
          we fly by our own mettle
                with words that count
Much as friends
         and with a heightened sense
                 of where it all ends.

Some Meanings of Silence

It has the last word so many times.
One takes his journey or performs his experiment
then arrives at silence,
apparently
a happy ending.
Silence at its most literal I experienced once
in a northern forest.
I marveled at it and felt misanthropic.
When bark fell or some buzzy flyer aimed by,
how exact.
Other silences just clutter the picture.
They mean "empty" not "clear."
They imply "flat" not "tranquil."
They say, "Step easily out this door, I'll carry on."
In the silence I know, I hear
how noisy my head is
and I shift toward conduct most efficient
at the still centers.
Snow knows this,
mold and mosses and mushrooms work this way.

Silence shapes out from inside,
it is not a way out,
not for the fatigued.
Peace may be the world widest awake, creation to be awake in.
The automobiles never cease on the highway below me.

The War Surplus Store

The man in the war surplus store said you had to lie
In the twenties when he sold shoes to women
With greater-than-size-five feet. Now he sells
To us the men's clothes, clodhoppers, and creels with a mature
Sense of honesty. He says his boss tells him this is
Not a high-class store.

But what a cheap
Good life it could provide: mattresses—thin,
Black and white, stacked dailies; or hammered beefsteaks;
Baklava or weighty tortes—buy one and sleep
Or imagine you own all its likenesses. Here is a buxom
Cubic "pillow" with a slit to accommodate even a large head
Tired of traffic (yet I can't imagine backwards
To what it genuinely is).

A frayed signal flag . . .
Certain prayer-rags a Missouri radio revivalist sends
For a considerable donation.

Towards the back the must
Thickens, towards the corridor dressing room between vet-
eran banner
And window. From there one can spy the boss,
Nosed and moustached like a Greek fisherman though wear-
ing a pink
Blotched sailor hat, camouflage if he fights
In rhododendrons. How good to be counted among
The surplus, the extra like cream that never reached bottom.
So the khaki is worn out on women and workingmen
And we pay only small prices for items from the tables
As numerous as the States.

Three Hard Sonnets

1

If you can buy all those groceries
why do you wear those clothes?
the woman said.

The phone rang:
If you answer our
question you can take a trip.

What do you think of me? said
the gambler telling me
his life.

Are you lost asked the policeman.
Why don't you smile.

No.

She said, Sometime I'd love to talk with you.
He walked out the door without saying good-bye.

2

I parked in the driveway.
Getting out I glimpsed the body
of a tall Indian brave
framed on the floor of the station wagon.

Another time one of those big family dinners:
we invited Uncle George
and he hooked over the table
from his seat at its head.

She sewed me a red dress but said
finish this hem,
I'm going away.

An old corpse of myself obstructed
our stairwell. I covered its face
with papers and books.

3

Proof! proof! It sounds like something
going up in smoke, abracadabra
smoke, producing
the answer to nothing.

At ease! at ease! You must look
at ease. There are places for nervousness:
stand trembling over the wastebasket
till anxiety falls in.

Beautiful! beautiful! I have no
big toe, no knee.
Compliments buried them
as well as insult.

Action!
OK enough, enough, wrap it up.

Homage to John Clare

If John Clare gave a reading of his poetry
what show would he put on, what clothes?
He would soon be escaping to his realest world.
He would need shoes.

We would not let you alone, John-bright
Clare-lunatic, and might you like that,
not to be lonely, left, and every Mary
turning to your door?

John Clare John Clare I stole your portrait
from a library book. I put it over
my desk at Honeywell and during some night
it fell, it fell,

and the janitor swept it away. "Pastoral
poems are full of nothing but the old threadbare epithets":
we await one who loves, we bury him, we rediscover
the most intimate of poets—

too grieved to be called confessional. On pootys:
"Blackbirds and Thrushes particularly the former

feed in hard winters upon the shell snail horns
hunting them from hedge bottoms

and wood stulps   taking them to a stone where they brake
        them
in a very dextrous manner." There is no judgment
there, where birds and pootys are not people.
Simply what happens

is mad then it is sane again before you know—
you have come in smiling from the storm.
Each year in a row we were given Shelley, Clare, *Songs
of Experience*, Keats.

Then deaths of all the wild and melancholy:
when Clare dies at Northampton 1864, Yeats is born
the next year. Would this age be kinder
or would we confuse

you on what you love? You blessed your two wives.
"The man whose daughter is the queen
of England is now sitting on a stone heap
on the highway to bugden"

penniless, with gnawing stomach.
I go out into the sunshine with his green book
and sit on the stair and say with a reader's silliness
John Clare is here.

Three from the Market

1

Come, radishes, rosy against your greens,
crisp when I am soft with weakness.

Oh what voluptuaries you are! yet
with the definitive sharpness of the scissors.

Ambition dances about you,
yet you are totally unmoved, like true

emissaries of red.

I, what there is of me, may be argued:
but you may not. Your whole self struts;
your leafiness flutters above your head
like a crown of doves.

No radish was ever terrified.

How you cheer me, strong souls for a dime.

2

I count 12 sections
nearly always, or average,
and buy Coachella grapefruit just to tabulate
12 until my refrigerator rolls with them
like model atoms
whose number is 12.

That's magnesium
of the intense white light.
Grapefruit's white energetic light
befits it as a morning dish.
Count 12 in the morning
and half the day is light.

But have you seen them grow
in the mineral white deserts?
More light more light.
This is the composition of grapefruit:
34% rind, membrane, seeds;
the rest is light.

3

O sad grapes,
sad as Chavez's eyes,
weighted with the very press
of holy tradition,

if I used to savor
even your rotting ones,
each with a different phase
of flavor

like waning moons,
you'll have to pardon me.
I must have known in my dreams
of the coming, voluntary

famine.
They say GI's have developed
a sudden taste for you,
O innocents.

But I imagine you on my table,
green on it, fresh and new.
Someday you will not need to bring with you
the knowledge of good and evil.

A Pumpkin at New Year's

Heads were rolling down the highway in high slat trucks.
I knew it was time to buy you and found you,
The last sphere unscarred and undistorted in the store,
Big as my own head.

It was time too to leave you uncut and full-featured,
Like the grandpa of twenty-five pumpkins in my past,
Khrushchev-cheeked and dwelling on yourself,
Great knee of my childhood.

I plainly thought you would rot.
I remembered the fetor of other pumpkins,
Their blue populations coming out of hiding as if at the end
Of some apocalypse.

I devoted a day to reading up on minor cucurbits:
I learned your dozen names in African
And came home ready to raise or raze you,
Positive of change.

But so far—eternity. I think I would not like
Eternity, after I had used my senses up,

As I've tried with you—fingertips dragging over your world
Pole to pole

Till they go dead like explorers, nostril cilia
Detecting your fragrance more delicate than they—
And my patience. It's Christmas, it's a new year
And I hear

Of a family who's kept you for four . . .
You endure like matter manufactured
And indeed your stem seems punched into your orange
      gathers
Like a button in a mattress.

Shall I give you a room or a shrine? And shall I
Purchase you a mate and family,
When ours is so inadequate, fixed upon your window
Deathbed as we are,

Centered upon a time and birth, new holiday, new friends,
New pumpkins, celebrating when all
That has failed us has passed away.
You have not failed.

Selective Letter

Embarrassment, foolishness, and fear,
Two hundred thirty-eight buttercups,
Rain and tea—

I write a letter:
> Dear Z . . .

I'm at the beach,
Pocketing shells and agates,
Swinging a walking stick that goes chg chg beside me.
Where you see that point
The town Bay Ocean washed out.
Shags fly and a heron's stuck in the shallows
Lettered with snags.
In small fire-green firs by a lighthouse
Goldfinches jerk.
And in the surf a couple in wetsuits
Tear crabs' claws off
And let them go.
Blond sea lions scoop themselves up on those ledges;
One partly decomposed pup dozes
Where the dunes rear up.
The proudest bouquet lies on the cliffs:

Salmonberry, salal, wild iris, wild rose—
Biting wind.
And my three
Black ships on the horizon . . .

        My dear Z,
I am really home again
Trying to get some sun
On the front steps.

When I think of you it is with
Embarrassment, foolishness, and fear.
And so I count the buttercups,

238,
Through showers of rain
And I have even spilled my tea.

Letter with a Black Border

Black centipedal bugs
Round the corner of a feather,
Turning their bodies like silverfish—
Otherwise they might be buses
Disappearing down a dark street.
To them it is crow city,
Pinions that may last as long as a building.

I could mail this letter there.

I was going to send you the green trees
But they were shaking.
I wanted to give you the wheat fields of Washington
But the Whitmans were massacred.
And the rattlers took everyone
The long way home.
And the squirrels ran down
Like snow in spring.
All of the rivers had battles;
I wanted to send you the trees
That hid the heroes.

The wild mint sends its own purple message
on runners.

Along an elegant white rib one vermin goes
Like a hearse over the bridge
In the city.

Its lights are on
But you do not know
A single one of the mourners.

Raffaele Minichiello

To steal from those that steal from you,
rise through the democratic process
and hold thieves dangling. Hold
your liquor well. Have your carbine
in such perfect condition in your brain
all thoughts won't trigger it. Hold it
so that no one knows it is there.

It is there. I suppose it is dark.
They do not paint carbines
the color of fresh fruits or Italy.
I suppose it is practical, suppose
I need one too, have one. Yours bloomed
into existence because you did not want
to stand trial, because you could not
stand America, because the homeland
of your mind does not stand for something
it isn't. For this you stand
all the way to Rome.

                    1966:
when you polished fruits for shelves
in Seattle, I bought them.

When you were trying to learn
the language, so was I. 1969: you're
in everybody's sky, you're the good man
escaping to good—or to jail.
You smile if the words of law escape you.
Please, to be free draw no gun, draw breath.

Marlow and Nancy

I am wondering how I could have changed her blood,
Physician phasing a baby's blue to red,
When I have no skill. My knife I thought
Was just rain's shine on stone. I killed her
Because she was alone, and in the night
The rain, its swallowing sounds, became cold people
Running me down into the softened earth.

                                    I heard a cat
Bite bones in a shrew and couldn't eat.
When my hunger left I still needed food.
So I moved as a cat, with my balls swinging.
She was bottomless in a way. She had antlers
In her from a fighting lover who died.
They hit my edge with a ring echoing their wilderness.

She was bottomless as a cloud
Because she could float
And put her arms around me. That is how
I might move my hands in her like dulled blades
And feel the sharpness in myself that she knew.
I thought she would drown me, then I could sleep.

After, it was as if I'd simply given her change—
In silver, paid her by giving her nothing.
Because I am returning to the earth,
I must stake my life with shrews, antlers, rain and stone.
I feel I am the river bottom between debris
And depths that will never know I balanced here
At this light point in a body
Pushing me away but blue, so blue.

Butchery

They're like the valentines from old schoolmates—
We were going to love each other forever.
Now I turn the beasts in the fields under my hands
And slice
Against the grain.
The table settles,
On meats, its earth.
A raw piece: fat skims it like the froth on beer.
I hammer it.
Something for the family, O our
Solicitous eunuch.
I like to think of the green fields where steers revolve
Beneath such a blue thumb,
Their hoarse announcements seeming never to express
       despair
Or more specific sadness
Than that the sky is darkening.
I can feel their necks breathe
And see their sides slapping like heavy suitcases.
Belly within belly now
We lie down to sleep,

Dull with each other.
I have washed the cutting board,
I have dried the fine knife that it will not rust,
I have scrubbed knowing the smell will stay on my hands
A few more hours, like perfume or gloves.

Peter Rabbit

Mushrooms grew near the tree
Nearly black with foliage.
Each footfall was a special touch.
Mother Rabbit wore a carrot-
Colored jacket and a broad purple skirt,
She was beyond hopping.
Over her paw a basket; her forearm, umbrella.
No no no! we're waiting for her to demand.
She looks that way though kind.

Father father's in the pie.
It was an accident.
It was a stupid way to die.
Peter knows how to be very naughty.
There is a shimmer
About the lettuce, French beans,
Radishes, and parsley—
Of evil or of humanity.
Peter is a thief.

Peter my hero I am a thief.
Peter I am a child.

Peter was most dreadfully frightened
And shed big tears.
Mr. McGregor was upon him
With his size huge shoe.
Of course we are going to win.

Lippity-lippity we wander
With puzzled Peter
But I don't want the story to be over.
They will make us wash the green
From our hands and our knees.

Cinderella

When she came to the mirror it was to her
Instrument of change, every scene in it
Total background, and her hard looking
Asking only to be plumbed the depth
Of a diamond needle, the broken in her
Still breakable as if new. A red line rose
And fell between images of dawn
And sunset . . .

               This was the dream room,
That had been lived with and never opened.
Everything in it was imagined, the curtains
The color of Chinese skin, with large printed
Purple blooms like distant ferris wheels
At dusk. At night the stars used themselves
Up on the rug.

Footsteps sounded
Into many years. Now someone enters
By the window. She turns, quiet.
The temperature drops. On the sill she finds
The alchemical gold ginkgo leaf and it fits
Perfectly the foot that she puts down
Gently on the beginning of autumn.

Sisters

She suffers like a red stone, small as a carat.
Her edges show cut to the women crying "Birthstone"
Beside her bed. She needs no mind for you
To see her this way, in a stainless setting,
White meticulous craftsmen turning her. She's been
Years in this Smithsonian and you want to steal her,
Your fine sister, and hang her on your neck . . .

                                            Pearl,
I want no one to find you so! With all
Your appearance of a rich woman, dressing in silk
I cover only my head with, the unraveled *Bombyx mori*
At the other end of the hole dug through to the orient,
Dug through; hard as you are, as the oyster is soft;
Black-pearl, natural-silk-dun, gray-matter vision;
Charity and investments; your skin now
Hangs loose as layers of beads around your throat.

We walked through dimestores and Penney's: you were
Younger. You bought me underwear and taffeta
For dresses with an erotic rustle, so I could stand
On the diningroom table while you hemmed—

Pins and scraps, scissors and punishment. She never
Favored me, an aunt, in the small house behind your large.
I lost a peridot ring in her garden.
You would find it, wouldn't you? And when I caught you
Clean as a cake tester in your slip, you blushed
And bawled me out.

               No, her heart didn't break you,
Nor your forgotten name, nor the mine made for her.
You can still give the gifts I knew you for,
In dizziness, in high blood pressure. Still, you fail
A bit. While she sleeps you count her, figure
Of a sisterhood in which you are not quite yourself,
Count and put in place like hand-sewn jewels
On your sweater from Hong Kong.

Peddler

The man vending needles at our door
Was lucky to greet you.
He looked poor but you acted needle-poor
Where I'd have said, I don't need . . .

He sells needles to prick your heart
And they'll take small bites
Out of my finger in a layer of skin
Where my feelings are thin.

The old thread knitting together his many wools
Might last another trudge
To our porch: he came last year but I
Refused and barely looked him in the eye.

I've lost how many needles since then?
Besides he is mute
And would see how dumb we are to buy
Three hundred needles for relief.

But he supplied us to the end of life.
I'll give away some.
And you might never use these points
That push through cloth, cut to be made one.

Coin

Wrong is the right word,
It'll do.
I don't make any mistakes,
Absolutely.

When I write a page
It's flat as a shadow.
When I need you
I never let you know.

Told you're wrong
You need two eyes
You can see deep into
To trust that judgment.

And if you see that deep
You love.

You love others
But you hate yourself.
That's right.
Whom should you hate?

Claiming your failures
You don't reclaim them.
You are loved.
Am I saying the right

Things about you?
You who count to me
Like all the lost
Right whales

Who may swim yet
In your tears and perspiration.

for Henry

Siberia

1

Remote,
as an ambition to join the circus.
When coming true is only a return,
powder over the footprint,
then I suppose one is no longer an exile
but merely remote
and strangely content
with his ambition
to be exceptional enough
for the circus.

2

It can be seen
if you hold your breath.
And likewise if you withhold
your thoughts.
That sapling doesn't appear in the air,
grown from the top down,
a nerve system in frost.
Breath is all a change within you,

the same change,
that shows what newness means to a man,
same newness:
one continues his life as originally.

3

A scene that does not admit
of a rare circumstance
is all distance.
On the streets, then,
we have law.
And for our own discipline
learn dance.
Where you are distinct
is close,
you watch a reindeer
nip young plants under the snow,
chew and swallow.
You desire that your removal
be no less intimate.

4

Were there a king still
his realm would be here,
unnoticeable royalty
and cruelty
awash in the massive politics
of the poor-as-snow
recognizing each other's glint.
But there is no king.
The earth opened up for him
and he replaced
metals
to be refined.
Crude king, crude metals,
crude as ice before snow.

5

Light
and the years it keeps flooding,
open tide,
vacant monument.

And so I shiver, yes, sometimes,
because the light is so broad
like an animal's back,
hard working,
cold,
a small harvest of wheat.
When the knife cuts
through the gray loaf
I feel I could be dawn
with its general tenderness,
dressing a continent,
meeting an eye.

6

It feels as if the ocean is near.
One stares into the possibility
of its expanse.
You are a small boat cut loose.
Wherever you go
is deep.
Flow? Influence.
The loved one's arms

that have to be crossed,
peripheral seas.
The setting out,
landscape in a skin.
Numbness:
ability to keep a secret
from pain.

7

What you labor over,
astute between walls
thick as classics,
your smoke,
your computation,
would seem to occupy all directions
you believe a man can move in.
The snow light
smooths the skin
and you are able to live out
your enormity,
with the example first
of green tree after green tree,
then with their blessing.

Eschatology

I accompany this life's events like a personal journalist:
"Little did she know when she got in the car that after-
    noon . . .";
or "Despite inauspicious beginnings,
this was to be their happiest year."

Little did I expect that our horoscopes would prove true.
And how could we foresee an answer to
that frankly secular prayer, we with so little faith
as to be false prophets to our most fortunate gifts.

I am glad when doom fails. Inept apocalypse
is a specialty of the times: the suffering of the rich
at the hand of riches; the second and third comings of wars.

Shouldn't we refuse prediction
that the untried today is guilty, that immeasurable
as this child's hope is, it will break tomorrow?

Poem for Ishi, the Last Wild Indian

1

As they put me to sleep, I could have died without pain
Or ever looking back, as if death were really unexpected.
It was black with no pictures, not the black of
Old shoes. I hadn't a scrapbook or a civilization
That kept busy with dreams. I knew nothing of the wall
I made stretched out in my due dark horizontal.

When I awoke, as if waking were more than what is
Necessary, I was a traveler with bare feet,
Braided hair, and a few possessions in a hospital drawer.

2

I hunted for someone to ask, whose time had starved
Before he lived and died again, What do you have,
Coming suddenly where all things are? Ishi,
I was reading how you took perfected silence with you
When you walked. When your own exposed body's bear
Brought you to sleep, the few things you owned
You also took: the bow's ache; its string, your singing
Brother; the arrowhead's small slope and humanity's point

Some whispers are so dumb they take eyes for ears.
Ishi, smoke tells everyone you've come from sleep
As it thins itself out almost into color.

Water Poems

1

There were no drawings on the page
only words
that no student was likely to explain
until to some stone like a drowned throat
one attributed certain meaning.

You step into the water
and it is those footprints
I want to recall
with these words.

2

The eternal tug
with its worth all behind it.
Here is evening's infantile blue gray,
the swords begin
to appear in the water.
The king is honest and thoughtless.
Where I am
is cast out of his eye.
What if I thought love grew?

He held up the stones
of smooth
diminishing proof
that cool strong houses
and rouse minerals
into the sunset.

3

Here's where the ships are expected.
So it is a place for you to begin
going away.

The days leave from here.
Why not my little pressure
evaporating from your hand.
The sea is postureless.
You'll be the back
of its mirror
like the moon.
This is where the sailor
asks no one permission
to come home when he's ready.

The land without scenery
where you, if you were mine,
would not be allowed to move.
But I am yours.

4

Their shapes are new eyes for the blind.
I need their luminous yes.
They are egrets.
Empty boats
in the dark.

5

The serfs with quiet eyes watch with the kings.
How can I watch for you,
invisible as the dead?
We are shadows on the tide
that the moon brings
high and low.
When you arrive empty

I realize too
I have said nothing.

6

I saw the net Ishi made.
Its knots are so evenly arranged
I know I am not a net.
My loneliness passes through a net.
How can a man find his food
in a place that won't hold his breath?
For a fish
it is not home either.
It is the net of lost happiness.
Why have I seen it?
Look at it.

Seaweeds

I know a little what it is like, once here at high tide
Stranded, for them to be so attached to the bottom's
Sarcophagus lids, up to their brown green gold wine
Bottle necks in the prevailing booze, riding, as far
As we can see, like a picnic on a blanket.

Whatever plucks them from below the red horizon
Like snapped pulleys and ropes for the pyramidal effort
Of the moon, they come in, they come through the breakers,
Heaps of hair, writing across the beach a collapsed
Script, signers of a huge independence.

Melville thought them pure, bitter, seeing the fog-sized
Flies dancing stiff and renaissance above. But I
Have eaten nori and dulse, and to have gone deep
Before being cast out leaves hardly a taste of loneliness.
And I take in their iodine.

Some Engravings of Pierre Joseph Redouté

The Exhibit

Lions outside but engraved lilies within.
Corms on paper and the growers assembling up high.
He held the lilies in sea light
Through that breaker, the day,
Green and white savages,
Like a girl studying gorillas.

Lily-of-the-Valley

These white brass bells,
Fingers after a meal,
Loose hair of a schoolyard noon:
If they keep a bed in mud,
While they stay on this white paper
I wipe my autumn shoes until they are museum pieces,
The galoshes of a bride.

Iris Xyphioides Rhizome

The bulb's clock, its Foucault
Ticking and knocking
Against the sternum,
Shows each solitary hour out,

My grenade of iris blow-ups,
Skies drooping incommunicable parachutists.

Tiger Lily

A rabbit's eye on the tablecloth.
Like fallen thrushes beneath the birdbath,
Tiger lilies have something to say,
Spitting in the overflow like skewered lamb,
For the sinlike.
These are as old as I.
These grow speckled as spaghetti,
They smell of garlic and gin,
Almost as uncouth
As a spinster (will there be
A revival of interest in her?),
If it were not for concealing
Their teeth.
If I kiss you,
I've kissed perhaps the strain itself.

Ferraria Undulata

Nurseryman,
I'd like something to embroider

The plaster cast behind which my house
Itches and knits.
What about the swallowable crocus
Or your black-blue mirror
Ferraria undulata,
Its spotted health?

African Iris, White, Yellow, and Blue

The glacier wants you
But it melts on your doorstep.
It's best withdrawn
Like messages into postal bags.
Its flower combined of
The long and the short,
Six touches like the insect,
A natural explanation
Of night and day on its shoulders, your shoulders,
It lasts a day
Like so little else that lifts a head.

Ballad of Sonnets

Loss is more dignified than abandonment, Madam
shouting *Roger* at the one lit window
in the office building

And to bring abandonment on yourself
is only a plum when you have plotted well
to muffle your cruelty turning another out

He will not throw the key down to you
You will not throw a rock through his glass

Take my advice, go home, and lock yourself in the lamp
and throw your children down the stairs
and listen to the bored patience of the trees

Raise one little aster for spring
For winter, let the bird drive its beak into the berry
Widow, turn black

*

Come my fluffy tousled owl
and let me lick your bullet wounds

Let's stay together, though you're dead,
I'm alive

And you little cousin Tommie J.
who shot your way
you Dick D.
who wanted to sleep with me

then wanted too deep
a sleep
And Ardis drop of honey
on death's tongue

I remember you fussing with your hair
and wondering what to wear

Wanting a Mummy

I've always wanted one,
A connection,

Leaning against the bureau, an in
To atrocious kingships,

To stone passages,
Those nights carrying the planets of the dead.

I'd like being able to ask it,
How do you like the rain?

Are you 3000 years old or still 25?
And to hear it replying,

Voluble with symbols
And medallions.

There we would debate, faced off
Across the room,

My room-temperature friend and I,
I with my hands like peaches

And my friend all
Shortbread and roots.

Collapsars

*The problem with
black holes is*

She would see
if I had a problem.
She read my birth
and I grew cold.
The chart held a "dark time"
for a "near" woman
in the snow stars of Christmas.
No, I said,
tragedies like that—

*there is no way
to see them
or hear them.*

As one hears
even in sleep
a man shouting Fire!
in the street.

They are stars
that have collapsed,
suffered what

even hard winter
doesn't bring:
snow fallen between houses
like a body
between bed and door.
Inhaling then choking

is called an implosion.

Without realizing
what happens,
you reach intensity . . .

The matter
in such stars
has been squashed together

like a victim
of a fire
carried down in a bag,
half size,
but then again and again,
fire after fire,

> *into forms*
> *unknown on earth,*

because our knowledge
has made us rare
and cold. How
can I look at it,

matter so dense
its gravitational field
prevents any kind
of radiation
from escaping.

I have kept my body heat
in heavy sweaters
and weatherstripping,
while earth's night grows colder
and what was burned
freezes.
      From that body
could a soul be escaping?

                              You couldn't see one
                              if it was right
                              next to you;

Miss Nugent was like that.
She must have walked
right by our house
twice a day. I never
saw her, never saw
her take the steps
one by one up to her apartment
after work and switch
on the light.

                              if you shone
                              a light on it

today, in the noon
after the fire broke out
like the sun's own rooster
rising from her window,
way too early
in the dark holiday morning,
licking up story after story,

> *the light would*
> *simply disappear*

like a Christmas present
we missed
and sifted the ashes for,
thrown away with its wrapping,

> *into the black hole.*

And what spark doesn't
desire all? And what
kind of star
visited a woman that night,
thirty-five,
of a secretary's passions,
ninety-eight point six?

A Feast for Rats:
Old Japanese Print

Their leader—almost a shepherd!—
Cascades the precious manuscripts, the scrolls,
The pile of books that fan out, stairways
In a bombing,

And presses his bubonic mouth
To history or literature, taking from them
A jagged kiss to soothe his gums
And carry off like a princess.

The ruck of scions fawning in his disregard
Nip out a character or place crinkled feet
On the fine hand someone wrote in
But an hour before

In the revery of twilight—wrote destined
For total darkness. They do not know
What to take and what to leave—
So just a taste!

The temple bell rings a swath down the wall.
The thunder . . . it is late. The gross one turns
Lustrous eyes sewerward: off!
To his sepulchral abbey, with scraps.

Sonnet for Joe

When I tell you I would rather you describe a clock than
    time,
that the essence of your ocean sentiments is not the ocean,
I'm wondering if you would live if your feet got tangled in
    seaweed.
Write me the superstructure of water.

And now you drop your face. I see my mistake. You did not
    write
to contend. So it was the ocean in four dry lines
like seaweed from Japanese groceries that thickens and
    plumps
when ladled in water. Look, you don't even like it

when I give you some copies of ocean poems. You detest the
    sea
and its marketable herring, its common tuna, and starfish
always losing their legs. Think of the man

who fell from his fishing boat in the fog off Alaska. He
    heard the motor
slowly *trup*ping away, its cargo of vain fish under its wing.
    Think of
his widow who detests the sea, who lives beside it, who
    writes now to her friend.